HOW TO GET OVER A DIVORCE

HOW TO GET OVER A DIVORCE

Discover My 9 Keys To Navigating
A Separation

JANE VELASCO

MISIÓN

MISIÓN

How To Get Over A Divorce
Published by Editorial Misión

First edition in Spanish: December, 2022
First edition in English: May, 2023

Copyright © 2023 BY Jane Velasco

ISBN: 978-1-958677-09-4

I dedicate this book to my children, Boone, Roger, Tessa, and Maya.

CONTENTS

ACKNOWLEDGMENTS

I thank my children: Boone, for always being the noblest human being I know; Roger, for teaching me his perseverance to achieve what he loves; Tessa, my first princess taken literally from a fairy tale, the most sentimental woman I know; Maya, my second princess and my beautiful challenger to life. To my family in general for always being there for me despite their adversities. To my best friend, Rocío Ardón, who, despite the distance, is always there for me at any moment, at any time. To Ronny Segnini, my unconditional friend, for his trust, love, and his consistent support. To my friends, Cinthia Barajas, Vero Palomino, Delia Diaz, Xenia Cordova, and so many others who give me their unconditional friendship. To Patty Chavez, who always pushed me

13

and believed in my dream. To America Reyes, a super woman in every sense of the word, for her friendship and professionalism.

FOREWORD

As a psychologist, Gestalt therapist, and life coach, I think it is not an easy task what Jane has achieved by describing in a simple and practical way a process as complex as divorce. With the experience she has had in advising so many people going through a separation or divorce, and, of course, from her own experience, it gives her the authority to speak on this very complicated subject.

There are several stages that she describes with her own experience, accompanied by steps that, in my opinion, are fundamental in the process, both during and after a divorce. For example, zero contact is key, especially considering that at the therapeutic level, this is where the real emotional detachment begins.

Of course, as a psychologist, one of the most relevant steps in my opinion is to seek therapy. Ending a cycle like divorce means putting an end to a complete entity—that of the couple, experiencing denial, sadness, anger, rage, resentment, and detachment. It is finding oneself again; and during this entire process, the accompaniment of a specialist is required and incredibly beneficial.

In these recommendations from Jane Velasco, we discover what she has gone through on that cobblestone road and find something that will lead us to a state of humility. As the Greek poet, Sophocles, said, "Whoever has not suffered what I have suffered, do not give me advice." Let us heed the words of those who have already lived through it, let us learn from their experience and training.

Undoubtedly, Jane's experience of overcoming cancer more than once, as well as her ability and strength to get ahead with her four children, is an inspiration to many of us.

Accompanying Jane in her story allows us to understand that divorce does not only mean the end of a relationship or the dissolution of a marriage, but it is also the breakdown of a planned future, economic readjustment, change of status, broken dreams, sometimes the loss of in-laws or common friendships, the fear of thinking whether you will be able to love or be loved again, and the uncertainty of whether you will find a partner or whether you will be able to move forward. All this can be accompanied by a lot of pain, confusion, and anguish.

However, we can also identify with Jane's strength. With her experience, she invites us to create new dreams and new friendships, motivating us to seek to generate different possibilities for ourselves and to give new meaning to divorce as she did, freeing herself from all emotions and helping many people along their own journeys.

Thank you, Jane, for reminding us that when we dare to see our pain and embrace it, there we find our true strength; then it becomes our passion, which is not so much ours, since it will be at the service of others.

América Reyes
Psychologist, Life Coach

Facebook: @psicologiaenamerica
Instagram: @psicologiaenamerica
Gmail: psicologiaconamerica@gmail.com

INTRODUCTION

I come from a family of strong women, single mothers who inherit strength and educate with love. My great-grandmother, my grandmother, and my mother all spoiled me as a child... but my grandmother was the one who really raised me, and I owe the woman I am to her.

I am Jane Karmina Velasco, and I was born in East Los Angeles, CA. As a baby, I was taken to live in Guatemala, and at the age of six, I was returned to the United States where I studied my first years of school (pre-kindergarten to third grade). Again, I moved to Guatemala and studied for a few years, but it was in the United States where I finished my formal education because it was here that I finally settled.

If I look back on my childhood, I can say that I lacked nothing. I had everything I needed, including spankings and punishments, because I was certainly naughty.

Despite the adversities I faced, I was able to finish high school, after which I went on to study Tourism and Business Administration—technical careers since I did not want to study at a university. More than anything, I thought of a fast career and I believe it was a good decision because tourism opened many doors in my professional career.

When I completed my degree in tourism, perhaps following the pattern of my mother, my grandmother, and my great-grandmother, I got pregnant and later became the proud mother of a baby boy, who I adored dearly the moment he was born. Six years after the birth of my son, I met the man on whom I will focus the story I want to share.

The man who came into my life was dazzling. I considered him smart, even though he had no formal education. He knew how to carry himself socially in almost any environment; he had a charismatic personality and was always liked by everyone he came across.

I fell in love with him, and we got married almost immediately. We did not have a period of courtship or time to get to know each other. He had a son from a previous relationship, just as I had my son. So, we quickly got married and had two daughters together as our marriage flourished beautifully. He and I were the happiest couple imaginable. We hardly ever fought or argued and our relationship seemed like paradise.

I felt like I had won the lottery. My friends were excited for me. They always referred to us as the "perfect couple" because he and I really got along so well and everyone around us could see it.

Our marriage lasted ten years. The happy union of that marriage lasted nine years, until one day, I found out that he had been unfaithful. Then, all the happiness ended. I complained and tried to forgive him, but it was from that moment on that my nightmare began. It was the worst year.

When I discovered my husband's infidelity, it was as if I had woken up from a dream. I lived in a perfect world prior to this incident because my life was complete. He and I had everything: a house, cars, good jobs, a family.

Even if it was only emotionally, he always supported me. After a while, I realized that studying tourism was not enough, and taking advantage of his support, I decided to expand my studies, for which he did not contribute financially.

Life was still fabulous. We had a great time, traveling and enjoying ourselves. We even traveled by car with the children to Guatemala, and on several occasions, we visited and saw many places in Mexico. They were great vacations and we experienced them as a picture-perfect family.

I felt fulfilled. I considered myself a full and happy woman. My house was always neat and tidy, as well, because although I worked tirelessly, I never neglected my home. I always took care of it and my family. There was always food for him, clean clothes, and time set aside for us to spend together as a couple and as a family. I also ensured that the children were enrolled in after-school sports activities. However, when I found out about the infidelity, my whole world fell apart.

The depression was so bad that I quit my job. My last baby had been born just two months prior, and my grandmother had passed away months before. I felt as though everything was against me; it seemed like everything had come together around me like a nightmare of which the most painful part was my relationship status and conflict.

The world came crashing down, and at that moment, I thought I would never get over it. However, as time passed, I realized that it was not as terrifying as I made it out to be because I am still here. I am alive, and now, I live happily and peacefully. I have gotten over it, and today, I can confidently talk about what happened without having a lump in my throat. I can even joke about my ex!

I will tell you my story. But first, I will tell you about how I met my then husband.

I worked for an airline and he worked for a baggage delivery company. It was a specialized company whose job was to deliver luggage that, for various reasons, did not arrive at the airport with the passengers.

My way of being and living made me curious. For this reason, in each job I had, I tried to understand and familiarize myself with all the areas. So, when I worked for the airline, I started as a Reservations Department Manager, then I was transferred to the ticketing area. I went through the Check Department and then to the Lost and Found Department, learning weight and balance.

When I retired from that job, I knew all its ins and outs, and was able to train the staff that came after me. I even became a supervisor.

I met my husband when I was working in the Lost and Found department. I have to confess that I didn't have much time to have fun or distract myself. I was very focused on my work, to the point where I didn't realize the mistake I was making in terms of our relationship. I met him on a Saturday, and on Sunday, we were already living together. After a month, we were already married, building what for me was the perfect life.

My husband worked part-time at the beginning. But as our relationship progressed, he gradually stopped working all together. That forced me to look for another job to support the household expenses. So, not only was I working for the airline, but I was also working for Macy's, a clothing store, while also being pregnant with our first child.

Perhaps now that I have come to this part of my story, you are wondering, *"So, what was he doing all this time?"* Well, yes, I was the breadwinner for the family. It was always like this and perhaps I must admit that he, as a husband and provider, failed. But to me, he was an excellent father, and when my daughter was born, he took care of all the parental and household duties.

I remember that my only maternal task, so to speak, was to pump my milk to leave it with him so that he could take care of feeding our daughter. He was the one who took care of her, even at night. During the first months, he fed her and raised her, taught her how to go to the bathroom, and how to get dressed. He was an excellent father and I thought he was also an excellent husband.

Over time, our needs increased, and I realized that he could not hold a stable or full-time job. So, I thought of looking for a third job. I lived to work because at the airline, I worked from eight in the evening to three in the morning. Then, when I finished that shift, I went to work at my third job at a hotel, with a schedule from five in the morning to two in the afternoon. And finally, at three-thirty or four in the afternoon, I would go to Macy's, where I covered a four-hour shift. I had no time to spare.

My workday consisted of a total of 18 to 20 hours. Then, shortly after, the airline company I was working for decided to move their headquarters to Costa Rica, eliminating all positions for all staff, which forced me to keep only my position at the hotel and Macy's.

It was then that I received the opportunity to work temporarily in the city of Palm Springs, California, for the same hotel I was already working for. That change meant a considerable increase in my salary, but it also meant that we would be separated as a family. I decided to take the opportunity nonetheless, and so, my husband at the time stayed in Los Angeles with the children and I went to Palm Springs. On the weekends, he and the kids would come to visit me or I would go to Los Angeles to visit them. A couple of months went by like that, but I did not feel comfortable. I wanted to be with him and our children like we were before; so, I suggested that they leave Los Angeles and come with me, since he did not have the commitment of a temporary or permanent job that would tie him there.

In addition to my desire to have us all be together, Los Angeles had become dangerous, making it nearly impossible to live there comfortably. On a couple of occasions, my children saw the police beating people on the streets. On one occasion it happened that a killer ran from the scene and crossed our yard where he left the gun with which he executed his victim under one of our cars. Our son, then six years old, witnessed this, took the gun, and brought it to me in the bedroom. It was very shocking and caused us fear. I didn't want that life for my children. I remember another time when looking through the window at my six and eight-year-old sons, I noticed that while they were walking away, the two were lowering their pants to half of their buttocks like gang members do. I said to myself, "They are adopting bad habits and this could get them into trouble." So, all these events, in addition to my new job re-location, made our decision to move to Palm Springs as a family easier.

Our life remained the same as in Los Angeles, except that if my husband worked three or four hours a day back in LA, he wouldn't work at all in Palm Springs. He was never able to find a good job; he found odd jobs here and there, but nothing else. It occurred to me to talk to my bosses, the hotel owners. I was responsible for a chain of 150 hotels and was in charge of training the managers of each hotel.

I spoke to the owners of the chain and told them about my husband's situation, who had no education but was intelligent and had the disposition of a good apprentice. I offered to take responsibility for his training and performance because at that time, there was a vacancy at one of the local hotels. My bosses agreed and gave my husband the opportunity.

His training lasted a year, during which I taught him everything he needed to know. And although everything was going perfectly, exactly at the end of his training, he resigned from the position because—as was typical of him—he could not keep a steady job; however, he took advantage of the training he received working in the hotels as a manager and started looking for another job. Eventually, he found another job at a resort as a supervisor. I did not imagine that this event would come with so many consequences; however, it was with this change of employment that infidelity came into our lives. Or at least I thought so, because over time, I realized that infidelities were several and lasted all throughout our marriage.

It was during those months of transition between his jobs that I gave birth to our second daughter.

I remember arriving one day to visit him, bringing him gifts from the kids and his lunch. When I entered his workplace, I noticed that the girl in front of me was looking at me in awe; then, he came out upset and complained that I had not told him that I was coming to visit him. He asked me what I wanted, which seemed strange to me because he had never behaved that way with me.

Tying things together, I realized that he did indeed have a relationship with this girl. Shortly before, it was just a suspicion, but I had no proof. That day, after what had happened, I was 100% sure that they were seeing one another.

I went home, and in the evening, my neighbor knocked on the door. He was crying and needed help. The man was heartbroken. I offered him a glass of water to calm him down. As I watched him break down in tears, I thought something very serious had happened to him.

When he finally calmed down, he told me in a broken voice that his wife was cheating on him. I sympathized with him and tried to encourage him to move forward, but at the same time, I realized that my neighbor's wife was the same girl my husband worked with. I felt a pressure in my chest. I told my neighbor, "I don't understand what you're going through because this isn't something I've ever experienced, but I'm very sorry. Please, get it off your chest."

Then, my neighbor stared at me and said, "You don't understand?" And no, I didn't want to understand, so I held my position that I had never been cheated on. Then, the man insisted, "My wife is cheating on me with your husband."

I froze. The man went on to tell me his story—the story that also involved my husband: "Have you noticed your husband's fancy phone?

And have you noticed that he spends all day communicating on it? I saw my wife's BlackBerry, too. The two of them work together and I've seen the messages they exchange with each other."

As I mentioned, he was a very charismatic person, and on one occasion, he told me, "I told you that I found the neighbor working in a fast food restaurant inside a gas station and I offered her a job at the hotel." That's how the neighbor started working with him. On one occasion, we even opened our house to the neighbors and I still did not suspect a thing.

The neighbor continued talking, but my mind went blank. At that moment, I was studying the situation; I felt that everything around me collapsed. How is this possible? I thought about myself, about my life, when I was a little girl, when I told my grandmother that when I grew up, I would work for the airlines or be a police officer. Just minutes prior, everything was fine. But now, everything was broken.

At this time, I had begun studying at the Police Academy. My day started at three o'clock in the morning. I had to be at the Academy at four o'clock, and then I started work at nine in the morning. I spent the whole day out of the house, studying or working, and when he asked me to go out to eat or to dance, to the casino, or to have fun, I refused because I either had to study, had to go to the

Academy, or had to work. I would tell him, "You go and have fun" because I had blind trust in him. I was capable of putting my hands in the fire for him. I was sure that he would never betray me. Then, everything became clear to me. It was when he went out with the neighbors and acquaintances instead of me that everything started between my neighbor's wife and my husband.

My neighbor kept telling me about his findings and said the following: "Look, we went to the dance on Sunday and there, I realized that your husband sent messages to my wife. He asked her to wear a miniskirt and not to wear underwear because they agreed to hide from me for a while." I didn't want to believe what I was hearing. I was still in denial. I thought the whole situation was a joke, a nightmare, a lie. I kept telling myself, *This is not happening, this is not happening.* I even remember the baby, who was only a couple of months old, crying and I ignored her. I was practically in shock.

After a while, my neighbor calmed down and left. I kept thinking, *How could this be? No. It isn't possible.* I couldn't believe my husband was capable of cheating on me. Our life was perfect. We were happy.

When did things change?

When he arrived in the evening, I waited for him to fall asleep and looked for a way to take his phone. I hid in the bathroom and, to my disappointment, found the messages he and she were sending to each other. They sounded like excited fifteen-year-olds; they were very explicit in what they wanted from each other. I couldn't believe it. I found messages in the trash and also in his inbox! They spoke to each other with such confidence and desire, and they communicated all day long, because working in a hotel, they could arrange to meet in a vacant room at any time. Messages like: "Let's go for a quickie" or "Put this on" or "Leave your underwear here." I was dumbfounded. How was it possible that they had a relationship behind my back?

How was it possible that there was such a relationship, so full of morbidity? I had never had a relationship like this. He and I had been married in a church; our wedding was a dream. We celebrated it at Disneyland and threw the house out the window. It was so hard for me to read those messages and see that the man I thought I knew was a total stranger. I was unable to believe anything.

The next day, I went to his work to confront the girl. When I got there, I asked her to come with me to one of the bathrooms in the lobby. I didn't want to fight with her. I just wanted to talk. That's what I told her: "I'm not here to fight for that man with you; in fact, I'm giving him to you. But I want you to know that you did terrible damage, especially to you, because I found out about your relationship with my husband because your husband came to tell me. You are destroying your husband and I don't know if you will be able to save your own marriage." She was speechless and pale because she did not know that her husband was aware of the situation. I was determined and was not able to forgive my husband for his infidelity. The girl tried to calm me down, to convince me that it was all a misunderstanding. When she opened her mouth, it was to tell me that "the messages were just words and a naughty game for fun, nothing is real, we haven't done anything," to which I replied, "I don't play like that with my boss." However, I could not believe it because those words and messages did not seem like a mere game.

I came out of the bathroom and outside, I found my husband, who followed me and intercepted me to ask,

"What did you come here to do?" I told him the truth: "I came to make sure you are cheating on me with your co-worker. Yesterday, our neighbor, her husband, came to tell me what was going on between you. I saw the messages and I know everything. I don't want you back in the house and I don't want anything to do with you. You and I are through. We are getting a divorce."

He was stunned and started yelling at me, "You are crazy and paranoid." His words did not offend me at the time; however, I gave him a chance and said, "Show me your phone and let's look at the messages," to which he refused. I asked him again not to come home and left. Later, he tried to get into the house, but I had locked all the doors. Still, he found one that wasn't locked, and that's where he entered. It was awful. We beat each other up. I was hurt so bad that I ended up in the hospital. My cheekbone and nose were broken. I didn't press charges because I was about to graduate from the Police Academy and I didn't want my record to get dirty. Also, I was very ashamed. I didn't want anyone to find out what had happened. He left our home and never realized how badly he hurt me or that I had to go to the hospital to recover.

Fortunately, I'm one of those people to whom any little bump leaves bruises. So, when I went to the Academy with all my punches, it was easy for me to tell them it was from the previous training. No one said anything; they were already used to looking at me like that. None of my classmates questioned my appearance. My instructor was the only one who looked at me skeptically and said, "Rojas, please come." In his office, he asked me what had really happened and when I told him, I couldn't hold back the tears. It was very painful for me to accept that I had suffered domestic violence and I shared with him my plans to graduate and then put a restraining order in place. I told him that I had run him out of the house and that I didn't want anything from him. I even told him that I was thinking of divorcing.

My instructor advised me not to file a restraining order—not because I was excusing my husband for his ill behavior, but because I ran the risk of also having a restraining order filed against me, since I was not what you would call a "white dove." I had also hit him and, although a woman's strength does not compare to a man's, I had training, and that could be used against me, meaning my police career was also at risk of ending before it began.

The other issue of potential conflict would be our children, the one I had before I married him and the ones we had together. For those reasons, I did not file a restraining order; it took two months until he finally left the house. At first, he came and went to spend time with the children. I don't know how or why, but during that time, he convinced me to give our relationship another chance.

He told me that it was illogical that he was renting separately and that he was also giving me money for the children. He convinced me that things between the two of us had not been so bad anyway. I agreed, and we decided to try again. A couple of months later, he returned home; however, I now know that was the worst decision I could have made.

Only weeks after he came home, we fought about everything, and by then, he was accusing me of being unfaithful on the nights he wasn't home. He broke phones and computers, and not a week went by that we didn't come to blows. Everything I did irritated him.

So, a year passed of this, after which I confronted him again because in addition to everything that was going on in the house, he also continued with his infidelities. Many times, he didn't even return home at night, and if he did return and I questioned him, I ran the risk of provoking a fight. I knew that if I started to question him about his whereabouts, and he turned on the TV or the radio at full volume, then we were going to come to blows.

On one occasion, we went to a concert with a group of friends, and before the concert started, while I returned from the bathroom, I saw him kissing one of the girls that accompanied us from the group of friends. At that moment, I made the decision to separate and he left the house again.

I spent that whole year in the midst of violence and uncertainty. I couldn't take it anymore. I put distance between the two of us. The divorce process took four years, during which everything became a perpetual discussion. A coming and going of meaningless claims. The last straw was when I received a summons from the court because he wanted to take the children away from me—all four of them.

He accused me of being a bad woman and a bad mother. He made up lies about me, claiming I was a bad example for my children because I brought men into the house.

He said I was into drugs and every illicit activity he could think of. He threw anything negative that could be attributed to a woman at me, even claiming that I forced him to have sex with me in return for letting him see the children.

Reading that subpoena and the things I was accused of was very hard. I had to take a considerable time to calm down—one breath, two breaths, three breaths. I had to put the paper on the table and decided to leave it there for a while. I took a week before reading it again and in the end, I didn't know whether to laugh or cry. I didn't know whether I should be angry or rejoice. He used that lawsuit, which was only one page, to try to destroy my reputation.

Already calmer, after a week of reflecting, I took the paper and read it again because I had to respond. Line by line, I began to refute his falsehoods. My answer was eight pages long. The sheet he had submitted was not even written on a computer or typewriter; it was hand-written and looked more like he had done it with his feet—poorly written with spelling errors, a document that did not appear to be formal.

I became very angry because I knew the importance of

a document of this nature, yet he treated it like it was nothing. Didn't he know that by filing the lawsuit, it had become a public document in court? I knew this because we had been taught it at the Academy, and I said to myself, *How is it that this man went to court and allowed all these lies to remain there in the public domain?*

I felt both anger and shame because everything he said about me was lies. And being in court, it had all been recorded. So, when I answered the lawsuit, I took my time. I made sure it was long and clear enough for the judge to read and realize the reality of the situation at hand.

I guess that was the moment where I started having the idea of helping people fill out their divorce papers, so that what I was going through wouldn't happen to them.

I told myself that I could open a business where I could offer services of that nature. At that time, I already had a notary's office, and I also knew how to do accounting for taxes. I could include divorce proceedings, especially because I had a lot of experience based on how difficult mine was.

In the end, that was what motivated me to decide to help people, especially women whom a man would try to stain like my husband did to me. I knew that a lawyer, no matter how good, would never be able to feel the pain, fear and uncertainty that a woman is going through during those moments. On the other hand, I had lived it firsthand, which made it easier for me to help them. Of course, the knowledge and experience of a lawyer is not devalued, but I considered that my own experience of a difficult divorce could be more important to empathize with someone.

After I sent in my response to the lawsuit, I was given a hearing date, which I attended on time; however, my husband did not show up. So, the judge decided that he would give him another chance. The new hearing was set for a month later and I arrived on time again. And again, he did not show up.

He did the same thing at the third hearing, but by this time, I was very angry, so I went to the people at the courthouse, and I remember saying to them, "You are allowing yourselves not to be taken seriously because it is obvious that he is wasting your time by not showing up for any of the hearings." The judge asked me what I was looking for and I angrily replied that I had not even initiated the lawsuit; it had been my husband who had requested it.

Just to be clear, at that time, I already had the divorce decree and also had custody of my children. I did not need him to give me child support. If he didn't want to give me anything, that was fine with me. The only thing I wanted was for him to stay out of my life completely because I didn't want to see him in any shape or form. And so, it was agreed. I kept custody of the children and he was told that he had to pay $150 a month for the younger girls only, as the other two children were older.

In the time I have been divorced—almost fourteen years—he has only paid $150 a month for the youngest child, who is now 16 years old. The court told me that if he got a better job, I could request that the child support order be reviewed again, but I never did. I kept those $150 a month that he sometimes sent them and some-times didn't. Money was not important to me.

I must say that I never spoke badly to my children about their father, and I always told them that the problems

46

he and I had were between him and me and that they had nothing to do with it. I encouraged them to continue loving him, to respect him, and not to hate him or be angry with him because although he had hurt me physically and emotionally, which they had witnessed one way or another (especially the older children), the problem was still between him and me.

The only one who doesn't remember the conflict is my youngest daughter because she was very young when we separated, and after a few years, he disappeared from our lives forever. He doesn't even communicate by phone with his children anymore—not even on their birthdays—and we haven't heard from him for almost 12 years now. I learned about his life because we have friends in common and I found that he lives in another state and that he had married again.

Maybe people thought and still think that I am spiteful or envious because I never used the health insurance that he got us. I got the girls another health insurance and I took care of my four children on my own, even in difficult situations, like when my oldest daughter fractured her foot and underwent two surgeries. At all times,

I took care of the expenses. I never used his money or the resources he made available to me because it was the only way I thought I could get by, not taking him into consideration.

Even though it has been a while since my divorce, I can still feel strong emotions when I remember the circumstances and situations that took place. However, my emotions are no longer as great and, although I still feel that impulse to cry with anger, it is now possible for me to talk about what I experienced.

When I was still freshly divorced, it was impossible to talk about the situation calmly. When anyone asked me what I felt when I spoke with the woman with whom my ex-husband had been unfaithful or what I felt when we tried again, I was not able to articulate a word. I was very angry and confused because one part of me refused to believe that he had been unfaithful to me, and the other part realized the reality. And both situations were painful. In the end, what was broken by his infidelity was the image I had. I thought he was perfect; my anger and disappointment came from the fact that I had given him all my trust but he betrayed it.

Over time, I realized that for my children, the situation of infidelity that I discovered after so many years of marriage was normal. My children believed it was normal for their father to be with other women because it happened all the time and I never noticed it. So, it makes me even angrier because he made them believe that this behavior was okay.

Hardly anyone comments on the first time a husband hits his wife or what it feels like to be hurt by your husband. Getting out of our abusive relationship was difficult because he planted the idea that I was to blame for all his mistreatment.

He told me things like, "If you hadn't done this I wouldn't have hit you" or "If you hadn't grabbed the phone I wouldn't have broken it." According to him, if I hadn't done everything I did, he would never have hurt me.

The hardest part was realizing that, even though I had finished my police training and was aware of what was going on, I gave him power over me and my emotions.

He really made me believe that I was to blame for the beatings, and of course, the next day, I tried to please him. I was the most loving wife and did everything I could to ensure he was happy. I accepted my supposed guilt and not only asked, but also begged him to forgive me. Now, it seems incredible to me that, although I was trained to avoid blows, I never defended myself in this situation.

I was very afraid and the fear forced me to submit to him. I remember that the most I could do to take refuge was go to the room where the baby was sleeping. Once, I locked myself in with keys and he came in upset and violently broke down the door. "Who gave you permission to lock yourself in?" he asked. I felt like a fool because at that time, I also had to ask his permission to close the door to my room. He hit me and instead of doing anything else, I asked him for forgiveness. "I won't do it again," I said because my mind was so damaged that I totally bowed to him.

When the lawsuit came to me where he requested custody of the children, four years had passed since the divorce. Time had done me good. As I read through the lies, I thought, *Did I marry Brad Pitt without realizing it?* On the other hand, it seemed grotesque to me that he said so many false things when, in fact, I had only supported him. When we met, he was undocumented, and when we got married, I was responsible for his papers. Thanks to me, he had become an American citizen. He was from Mexico City, and after our divorce, he began to travel there a lot to visit his parents, and sometimes, when he couldn't find a place to live or a job in Palm Springs, he would go to Mexico City for six or eight months at a time, then he would return and restart the custody process. Then, the lawsuits would start all over again.

The lawsuit in which he accused me of everything unimaginable came at a time when he hadn't seen the children for eight months, so it was ridiculous that he complained that I was asking him for so many things when we hadn't even seen each other. *Who was this man? Was he the same one I had married?* It's amazing how far someone can go to discredit another person.

I felt confusion and anger. It was clear what kind of person he was; I could tell from everything he was able to write about me. I was the mother of two of his children and had even adopted his oldest son, so I couldn't quite fathom how he could do this to me.

Between anger and dismay, I realized that anyone who knew the whole story would applaud me, for not only did I help him tremendously, but I also adopted his son and kept the best of him without hesitation, not because I expected applause, but because I loved that little boy with all my heart.

My children are a great blessing, and when we were married, neither he nor I made any distinction with our children. Then, when he left, he was the father of four children and he left all four of them. I wondered how he could leave everything behind like that so easily and at what point he had disengaged.

I also wondered how he came to demand custody and everything else when he had simply removed himself from our lives. It was then that I realized I was free of him because after all I had been through, I was able to understand that he was the problem.

After taking my time to respond to his lawsuit, I received

a response three months later. I didn't want to know anything more about him and I did not want him to come near me. I emailed him and told him not to insist on the custody suit because there had already been three occasions in which he had missed the meeting.

I asked him never to cross my path again, neither for better nor for worse. For me, that email was the point in which I could finally leave him behind and go my own way. It was at that moment that I could start with the famous zero contact, which is always so difficult for a thousand reasons, yet is recommended by experts. However, sometimes it cannot be done because between two people who have shared so much, there will always be something that brings them together.

Throughout my process, I learned many lessons. I learned that to heal, it is necessary not only to want it, but to also have some kind of support. I remember in the third hearing, where he was asking me for custody of my children, I had the idea of using everything that was happening to me to benefit other people. I wanted to help people who were going through a situation like the one I was going through. I had this revelation—a clear idea of how to help people and also transform it into a kind of professional activity.

In fact, throughout my divorce, I had this concern. Divorce hearings are public and you are cited according to your last name. We were registered as Rojas, so between the letter A and R, there were many dead hours. Almost always, our turn came when lunchtime passed. I remember listening to all the drama of the previous cases, which made me think and reflect.

I learned the judges' words because every time I started a hearing, the judge would say, "I remind you that you are here because you could not solve your problem outside of court; however, you, at some point before this hearing, before you came to my court, loved each other..."

Those words undid me to the point that many times, after hearing them, I refused to continue with the divorce process because I wanted to believe that it was possible to rescue the affection that once existed between us. I think it took me four or five times trying to file the divorce to finally make up my mind.

There were times when, being in court, I would decide

not to give him up, go back to the car, and start crying, thinking about how it was possible that our marriage, which had been perfect, was ending completely in this way.

HOW
TO GET OVER
A
DIVORCE
IN NINE STEPS

In my business, I have two types of clients: those who want to be taken by the hand during their divorce process, and those who want me to advise them to answer a lawsuit in good terms.

For me, the client is the most important thing, and in both cases, I need to know their story to give them the right advice and service.

When my clients tell me their story, I can put it down on paper and tell the judge the reasons why a person wants to divorce, outlining the terms on which they want to do it. I can also explain why a claim should be disregarded or how it could be varied to make it more appropriate.

Every time I support a divorce process, I try to put myself in the person's shoes and apply my own perspective and experience where appropriate.

I once had a couple of clients who became my friends. They had met through social media networks and then got married outside the United States. He went to that country to get married and then started the procedures to bring her along with their child.

At first, he traveled for two years to see her because he had the opportunity to leave his business. He was always a very hardworking person and looked for ways to prosper; he owned property and found ways to increase his wealth and continue to grow. By the time they were married, they had enough to create a great patrimony, to the point that they had a very nice house and lived very comfortably.

However, since she came to live in the States full time, problems arose. I met her when she first arrived. He introduced me to her and we went out to lunch; we really liked each other, to the point where we became friends and even confidants. Both he and she felt comfortable talking to me.

When they told me their problems, I listened to them. Then, I told them, "Being married is difficult, but you are grown up now...you are over 50 years old. You are not two kids who didn't know what you were getting into." So, what problems did they have? Well, their problems were primarily financial in nature and were related to the business and the properties they owned.

He bought a house and left her off the title because he claimed that she had no credit since she had just emigrated. However, at the same time, he asked her to go to a notary to sign other documents. This did not seem appropriate to her, so she decided to contact me and ask about this procedure. I explained to her that she would be left off the title, but only for the purpose of qualifying for the house loan. It was easy because after the purchase, they could change the documents by going to the property authorities. Then, she would appear as the owner, too.

Everything was in order, but she still didn't take it well. It seemed to her as though something bad were going on and she lost confidence. She felt uncomfortable if she appeared in the title because somehow, she felt she was being deceived or defrauded.

I tried to persuade her. I tried to help them by giving them my recommendation on how the laws worked in the United States. I told them that when buying a property, it was possible that both people did not qualify. That is why it was possible to make this change, so that the house would go out with only one name and then the correction would be made without any problems.

The matter became so serious for this couple that in the end, he was the one who decided to file for divorce because he felt that she was not supporting him.

When she received the divorce papers, she was angry because the whole thing had been a result of her not wanting to sign those papers with the notary. Neither of them had confidence in the other.

Then, to top it all off, she reminded him that he had been the one who had brought her to the United States, since she did not even want to come there in the first place. According to her, she was fine in her country, but now, she was in a city she did not know, without friends and without family. Then, as he was asking for a divorce, she told him that he should offer her money for her support, since she was alone and without opportunities in a new country.

She told him, "So, now, in addition to being divorced, I am going to be homeless and without a place to live... well, no!" He told her, "I will not give you more money. I already gave you documents for you and your son; with that, you can defend yourself and work. You are still strong enough to do it. What's more, if you want, I'll give you more money in exchange for not putting anything into the divorce." She accepted, but wanted me to sign before a notary.

I prefer not to make arrangements with my friends and acquaintances, but this time, I agreed, even though I knew it could have been counterproductive. So, they came to the office to complete the documents, and I wrote all the details. Just as I was listing the conditions, which were that she would receive the agreed amount at that time and the rest upon signing the divorce, they started arguing. She did not agree to the deal and refused to sign.

I didn't know which way to turn or what to do. It seemed strange to me, since I had talked to her prior and she was in agreement; so, I didn't understand where all this commotion was coming from. Then, she very angrily said, "I found out that he is worth more than fifty thousand dollars." She now wanted a hundred thousand dollars to sign the divorce. And my poor friend didn't know what to do because he had no way of getting that amount of money.

The whole discussion had taken place in my office, and to be honest, I didn't want to spend the afternoon watching them fight and not being able to come to an agreement. So, I found a way to distract them and told them that my brother, who is an international auditor, was visiting and was in the next office. I asked them to stop shouting, as they were making a spectacle of themselves and it was embarrassing for me. They felt aggrieved, but continued to argue.

I asked them to let me know if the agreement was going to be made, since they had already been discussing the terms for half the afternoon. He said the following, "Okay, I'll give you what you ask for, as long as I divorce you already!" She agreed; so, he went to the bank and while he was gone, I asked her whether she was sure about everything.

The truth was that the agreement reached was very good for her, since she had obtained quite a large economic benefit, especially considering that she had only been married to him for two and a half years. And the fact that both she and her son had obtained legal residency in the United States thanks to that marriage topped it all off. I told her to sign everything without making too much of a fuss so that she could avoid court because if her case went to court, she would not win all that money. However, she had other ideas; she had contacted another person in her home country, who had told her that she was supposedly entitled to half of everything he had. I explained that this was a lie because the laws in other countries were different from those in the United States. I asked her if they had signed a prenuptial agreement, and even if she did, she would only get half of what was made during the marriage, not what he had before.

She became stubborn, insisting that she was entitled to half of everything.

My friend arrived shortly after with the agreed amount. They signed the papers and she left the house that same day. After a month, the next agreed amount was prepared, so there was only one last payment to make. I spoke to her and asked her to come for the check; she also had to sign some deeds for the property located outside the United States. She refused, but my friend had given me specific instructions that if she did not sign the deeds, he would not give her that check.

When I told her this, she got upset, argued that we were breaking the contract, and left very angry and determined. However, I tried to convince her to sign because it was all she needed to receive the money. She refused. My attempts to persuade her to accept the agreement were based on my experience and had nothing to do with the fact that they were my acquaintances, nor was I taking sides with either of them.

She decided to get her own lawyer, to which I had no objection since she was entitled to counsel of her own choosing. Between them, they planned to sue, seeking all the property as a divorce settlement. In their lawsuit, they argued that my client tried to defraud her because she did not feel confident that she would get the last payment if she signed the papers. As much as I tried to reconcile things and make her see reason to sign, I was unsuccessful.

I told her that he had acted in good faith by having

already given her an amount of money and that now, with the check for the same amount, he was also acting in good faith. All she had to do was sign the papers, but she still refused. She said she did not trust him and would not consent.

All this led to her case going to court. When the trial was over, she lost because she had no tools that would allow her to win what she wanted. I had warned her. I had told her that she could lose, but she didn't want to listen, and so, she could not get what she had already won.

The laws are different in each country, but the social contracts are always similar. In this case, she would have been able to take more than a certain amount and I gave her my own case as an example. I showed her how easily a divorce can leave us homeless or penniless. In contrast to me, she wanted money more than peace.

These experiences taught me to give the best of myself in my work as a divorce consultant.

I have been in this position since 2010, obtaining excellent results. I have also noticed that there are some strategies or keys, which we could also call secrets, that allow the divorce process and the subsequent processes to be easily solved.

My personal experience has helped me give this kind of advice to divorcees because dealing with them always leads to knowing them personally, and that requires advice and counseling from a personal standpoint.

Below, I describe these keys that I have discovered over the years to successfully complete a divorce.

STEP 1:
ZERO CONTACT

I believe this is an important point and one that is always difficult to conquer. It is surely easier said than done.

In relation to my divorce, this was an incredibly difficult point to apply, especially because my partner was conflictive, and chose to solve all our issues with violence. Even though I pushed for peace and calm discussions, for him, everything always included screaming and hitting. So, if you are having a difficult separation (or you already had one) and you want to avoid more aggression, zero contact is the best way to go.

This is the first step in the process. Do not have any kind of contact with the person. Do not call them, do not pick up their calls, do not email or message, do not look them up on social media, and do not indirectly hear from them through family or mutual friends. Nothing. Zero contact.

I believe that it is possible for couples to get along well after divorce, like the famous singers Mijares and Lucerito. In my case, although I had a complicated divorce, I still get along well with my son's biological mother. I mean, I get along well with my ex's ex. She has shared her reasons for why they are no longer together or why they never worked as a couple. She has always been very grateful to me for adopting and raising her son. She even tells me at times that she believes her son loves me more than he loves her, but nonetheless, she always expresses gratitude. So, I don't doubt that there can be relationships that, on different sides, work and manage to establish friendships.

I have a sister-in-law, my ex's sister, and that woman is a Godsend. She and I always had great chemistry, and we still connect on social media. Although I have completely zero contact with my ex-husband or with his family, I get along very well with her; she is a person I enjoy talking to and sharing aspects of my life with.

You can achieve this as long as you don't go digging for

information about your ex through these relationships. You should not inquire about third parties or intermediaries either.

This means that there are people with whom it is worthwhile to maintain contact and others with whom it is not. So, it is possible to have a friendship or to maintain a cordial relationship. As an example, I have ex--boyfriends, with whom, to this day, I can talk to and say, "How are you doing?" and everything would be fine.

I can even talk about their new relationships, their children, or ask them for favors. I have friendships with ex-partners, some of whom I even do their taxes. That is how I know that I am not a conflictive person; I can reach the point of having the maturity to greet these people politely.

As my mom said, "The cordial does not take away the brave." That cordiality that you have with the person, the education that you have, those are yours, you choose them. Everyone can choose with whom to be cordial and polite.

So, what do I advise? Zero contact. That is where we must begin the path to overcome a difficult divorce.

This person no longer exists. They are unknown to you. You do not look for them physically or in any other way. You eliminate them; you block them completely from your life, from social media, and from your phone. This was very effective for me. I broke contact even with people in his family and with people who were related to him. I believe that when you get married and when you get divorced, you also do it with the family. So, I never again had communication with his siblings or his parents or anyone else, with the exception of his sister, which came later when I was in a better place and able to draw clear boundaries for myself and others.

Something curious happened to me when I implemented zero contact because even though I knew our relation-ship was toxic, I hid my divorce from my family. I didn't want anyone to know that I was getting divorced; I was ashamed that people would think I failed.

I come from a very conservative family. I was the first to achieve everything I had dreamed of. I set an exam-ple for my sisters and cousins, and in the family, it was established that first, you had to study, and then you would get married, have children, travel, and everything in between. Divorce was never on the table.

My mother was the only person who had been a single mother, even after she got married, had other children, and formed a stable marriage; so, when I decided to get divorced, I felt ashamed to the point that when we separated for the first time, which was in October, just as the end of the year holidays began, I didn't know what to do. We are a partying family. At home, there are always get-togethers and we look for any excuse to celebrate.

I would arrive with my children and they would ask me about my ex-husband, to which I would reply, "Ah! He is working... He couldn't come today..." We were no longer together and I kept lying, saying he was busy. I was terrified that they would find out what was going on. I didn't even want to imagine what would happen if they did.

But one day, they found out, and one of my uncles, who was like my dad, told me, "Well, you've already decided to get divorced. The only advice I can give you is not to become the mistress." At that moment, I didn't understand what he meant. I thought, *How am I going to become the mistress if I'm the wife?* It didn't make sense to me.

But my uncle insisted, "That's all I advise you."

What did I find out later? Well, when it became easier for me to get back together with him, even though we didn't live together, I agreed to have meetings. It was then that I realized that I had become the mistress. I was no longer the wife. I became the lady-in-waiting and that was exactly what my uncle was referring to.

So, now I understand that when I wanted to implement zero contact, I couldn't do it because I somehow got back together with him. Zero contact can be a long and difficult thing. I was unconsciously looking for excuses to talk to him—about the car insurance, our credit, the children.

I spent four years like that until he sued me. But from that day onward, I never sent him a single text message, nor did I ever call his phone. He has sent me a couple of emails since. The last one I received was six or seven years ago. He wrote to me about something related to the girls' health insurance to which I didn't respond because I was already determined to apply zero contact.

Although it was difficult for me to get to that point, it was the lawsuit that got me to that place because it made me feel attacked in such a way that made me realize I was doing something wrong. And that was precisely the fact that I was not implementing zero contact.

When I finally decided to implement zero contact, it was the day my life changed. Sure, not all my problems were magically fixed, but my life took a turn where I was finally able to say, "Okay, now I don't have to contact this person for any reason."

During this process, I blocked him both on my phone and on social media because it is easy to be tempted to write hints or receive them. I discovered that divorce was something so private and painful that sometimes, it can't even be talked about, and reopening that conversation only happens little by little over time.

In this sense, I can tell you that people started to realize that I was divorced and then they wanted to know details, just because I had made a comment on my social media. That's how I learned that you should not tell anyone. If I hadn't posted anything, no one would have bothered me.

I also suggest, if possible, physical distance. I was able to put many miles between us that were very impactful. Also, getting away from social environments is very effective. To give you an example, shortly after my divorce, I had contact with a friend of my ex-husband. At first, I didn't see anything wrong with it, but it was only later that I found out that he was telling my ex things I was sharing with him. I stopped frequenting the same places I knew he attended or somehow would have attended because then I would know something about him again.

Sometimes, people ask me if I recommend that one of the two parties leave town. If you are experiencing a particularly difficult situation with your ex-partner, then yes, do it if you have the means! My ex-husband told me before I got divorced, "I have to go because if we stay in the same city, we will kill each other." When the lawsuit was finalized one or two years later, I never ran into him again.

A long time afterward, my daughters and I went to eat at a restaurant, and he happened to be there. We had to leave right away because I did not want to break the zero contact boundary I had set. The girls got upset. They didn't want to be there either. They told me, "Mommy, he is not even looking for us and he is there, laughing and talking." I did not want to hurt the girls, and I had worked so hard to maintain zero contact—I didn't want to break it over something so trivial.

When the court rules on how the exchange with the children will be facilitated, it gets easier. For example, in the United States, the court determines that the exchange of the children is done in a public parking lot. In this way, the couple does not even have to see each other. They just open the door for the children to change cars and the parents do not have to get out of the vehicle if they don't want to. This makes things much easier and happens when the court is involved. However, in the case that the court is not involved in the process, it is more difficult to find a neutral position.

If it were possible to have an intermediary to do the exchange of the children, it would be favorable because that way, the parties involved in the divorce would not have to see each other.

Regardless, strive for zero contact whenever possible. Although it may be hard at first, it is worth it in the long-run.

STEP 2:

ZERO
SOCIAL
MEDIA

Social networks have taken control of our lives. People use them more and more every day and their implications are increasing all the time. For me, for example, when I got divorced, I was affected by the hints I received about him through social media. By not blocking certain people from my social networks, I exposed myself so that they could see me and the reality of my situation on social media. In this way, when I posted things like, "I am a free woman. I am a single, empowered woman" on social media, instead of strengthening me, it hurt me because I let the world understand that I was divorced.

Now I could post these types of phrases, but having posted them at the time was one of the worst decisions I could have made. I would recommend to those who are going through a divorce that they only use social media for information, not to vent about their lives or to send hidden or indirect messages. Rather, use it as a means of distraction, entertainment, or connection with people who are truly worthwhile.

I even recommend closing Facebook and Twitter for a year if you can. This would be great. If it is not possible to close these accounts for various reasons, I suggest limiting their use to reading and being aware of what happens in your circle of friends. The important thing is to avoid sharing about yourself and to maintain your privacy.

There will be a time to share about this aspect of your life after the divorce process has been completed. As they say, after the storm comes the calm. So, wait for that time to come and then you will take up social media. You will be able to post a message or repost a little poster because you liked it without anyone thinking that you felt identified, but because you simply liked the reflection, the content of an article, or even a meme.

It is important that you let the process pass because during the divorce, you may be tempted to use social networks to unconsciously attack your ex. We've all seen that storm where someone sees a person going through a separation and is venting about what they are thinking and the emotions they are having. They expose their anger and they make videos saying inappropriate things.

I recommend that you not do this. The best thing to do is to look for a person you trust—a friend, a sister, or someone you can write to in order to unburden yourself. This is particularly what I recommend to all those who I help with their divorce processes. They often say, "Hey, he sent me this message and I answered him the following..." Sometimes, I read these messages and notice that in reality, the moment and the anger make them respond inappropriately.

Then, I advise them, "Look, don't write that. This can hurt you." I emphasize to all my clients that even a message can harm you legally. I tell them instead to send me the message if their partner happens to contact them again so we can come up with a politically correct response together. I say, "That way, you will give him a slap in the face with white gloves, but you won't make yourself look bad in the process."

I recommend that the person not do that, to change their language, their expressions, to be more direct, to get to the point and avoid being rude. And one of the main pieces of advice I give them is, "Don't respond with your emotions. Keep your cool, just like I did."

When I got divorced and answered that lawsuit, I didn't do it with my emotions at the forefront, even though I was very upset with tremendous anger. I put the lawsuit on the table and I said to myself, "In a week, I will answer." When that time passed and I read it again, I no longer responded with my heart, I responded with my head.

STEP 3:
SEEK DISTRACTIONS

The next step I suggest is to seek distractions; you just have to be careful with the type of distractions you choose because sometimes, it can be a double-edged sword.

When I divorced that man, I thought, Well, *I'm going to distract myself. I'm going out to a dance.* Surprise! He was watching me. So, he would show up and ruin my night, make a fuss, and I would have to leave in shame.

So, I stayed away from those distractions and preferred to lock myself in my house. As time went by, I was able to go out without fear that he would make scandals. I remember that on one occasion, I went to a concert with some friends and there was the girl with whom he had been unfaithful. When we left the concert, we went to a bar and that girl sat next to me. Our shoulders touched. She turned white when she saw me, but for me, it was the most normal and inconsequential thing. By this time, I was over the lawsuit. This happened long after my divorce had gone through.

That night, it caught my attention that she raised her glass and I saw that she was wearing my wedding rings. No wonder I couldn't find them! That's when I got cold. I thought, *How did she put my rings on just like that?* So, I said, "Are you okay?" She looked at me and said, "I can only tell you that it was a mistake to have been with him. We are no longer together."

It was then that I found out that before I started zero contact, he was already on bad terms with that girl. He would disappear without telling her. On one occasion, he went to Puerto Vallarta. I keep this in mind because my youngest child got sick, and I would call him and his phone would go straight to voicemail.

He and I still had accounts together and I saw that he was spending money in Puerto Vallarta. It seemed weird to me. Then, I found out that this girl was the one who had accompanied him on that trip. I confirmed this when

I saw her with my wedding rings. I no longer had that feeling of anger; it didn't occur to me to claim or say anything to her. The reality was that I was distracting myself. I went to a concert and that was it. Fate or chance put me in a place where I met her, but hey, it's part of life.

The distractions I recommend, which do not come with the negative consequences I just told you about, are activities that allow you to get in touch with yourself and reflect. Something that works very well is hiking or walking. I like it very much and I remember that I was looking for that contact with nature, with myself, and with my emotions. This moment of rupture can also be a moment of connection with yourself in which you get to know yourself again.

I went through that stage where there was a lot of code-pendency. I had insomnia and would wake up and open my eyes to try to guess what mood he was going to wake up in. I knew that if he woke up in a bad mood, my day would be lousy, but if he woke up in a good mood, everything would be more passable.

What happened after the divorce was terrible for me because I didn't know myself and I had to spend time getting to know myself again. From thinking about what I liked and disliked to making big decisions, like saying, "I'm not going to live like this—for someone—waiting to see how they are or if they are happy." And I think that's what the distractions helped me to do; they helped me to get to know myself.

I want to clarify something. Among the distractions, I do not recommend clinging to the idea that "one nail pulls out another." Notice that when I discovered my ex-partner's infidelity, I ran him out of the house and then went back to him and we separated again. During this, something very unfortunate happened to me. I would occasionally go out with a group of friends to distract myself. In this group, there was a guy—a good friend of both of us, lifelong and single. Anyway, he started to court me and made it a point to be there for me, my children and me. However, I didn't want to pursue anything serious. When I went to a concert with these friends, I realized that my ex was already dating another girl that we both knew.

That was the reason why I accepted the boy who was courting me. We became a couple shortly after. However, even though he was an excellent person, the relationship did not work out. Today, I still have contact with him and we are close. He is already married and has a family, but at that time, I understood that it had been a mistake to get involved in a relationship just out of spite.

I think I did it as a kind of revenge, which is an emotion that leads you to make the wrong decisions. Now I understand that I started dating this person because I wanted to get back at my ex, not so much because I was attracted to him. I wanted my ex to feel what I felt when I saw him dating someone I knew.

It didn't help me to have a new partner. Maybe with time, it can be convenient, but in the first few months—in the beginning stages of the divorce or separation—I do not recommend it.

It is best to stay away from new relationships until you know yourself well again, until you heal the wounds, until you have established that zero contact and are well with yourself.

The important thing in this first stage of the divorce—when it is about to happen or is in the process—is that you give yourself some time, go hiking, walk barefoot in the countryside or on the beach, and find a way to reconnect with yourself and with your emotions and feelings.

What I recommend is searching within yourself, distracting yourself from worldly affairs and problems, and finding yourself. This process cost me a lot of work, especially learning to do things alone. How to get to eat without him in a restaurant or how to do things I used to do with him became a completely new learning journey. Now, I can go anywhere by myself and I don't need someone to make me feel complete. I can go for a drink or go to a concert alone.

I recently had the opportunity to go to Mexico City, since I had been yearning for almost six years to go to the theater there. I went to see a play written by actors Odín Dupeyrón and Mauricio Ochmann. I traveled alone to Mexico City, went to the theater, bought my ticket, sat down to watch the play, and enjoyed it to the skies.

You can enjoy your own company and be at peace with yourself. Now, I enjoy myself very much in my own company. I can go to the gym alone, watch a movie, go to a restaurant, and travel. I currently have a partner, but today, I understand the importance of the space that my life and the company of a partner should have. We all like to do our own activities alone and it is necessary to grow.

Even though we think couples should always be together, the reality is that we all need to be unique individuals with our own hobbies, time, and space. He and I like to do things alone and there is nothing wrong with that. There is a very fine line between being in a relationship with room for individuality and being in a codependent relationship. You learn all this over time and by taking care of yourself. That's why I suggest distractions like walking, traveling, and engaging in activities that contribute to your personal growth.

Some people tell me, "Hey, for that I need to spend money," but the truth is that you don't always need a lot of money to travel. If you are organized and know how to manage your finances, you can travel without spending a lot. There are plane tickets for up to $100 and you can come and go easily on a weekend.

Dedicate time to yourself, to do or learn what you like. I like to travel, so I grab my little backpack, put two changes of clothes on and embark on a journey to see what happens.

STEP 4:

TAKE THERAPY

Many people think that therapy is for crazy people, but I don't believe that is true. When I talk about going to therapy, I don't necessarily mean going to a psychologist or a psychiatrist. There is a big difference between the two because with a psychologist, you only talk, while the psychiatrist can prescribe you medicine. But there are also therapists, who can help or guide you through difficult situations.

To date, I am still taking therapy because over the years, I have discovered that therapy is a tool that helps me with something fundamental: organizing my thoughts. If you can't do this by yourself or you are overwhelmed or don't know where to start, therapy can help.

A therapist is an instrument of self-help, who guides you by the hand: "Look, we are going to identify why you are like this, where your thoughts come from..."

I am not saying that only those who get divorced should resort to therapy; on the contrary, I believe that everybody should attend it in different situations—for work, family, or personal reasons. So, when there is a circumstance that is so upsetting, such as divorce, I suggest you go to therapy!

Sometimes, I have twelve-hour shifts where I start at six in the morning and finish at six in the evening. The day doesn't seem to catch up with me. I get stressed out and think, *Why didn't I make it through the day if I did everything on my list?* Then, I go to therapy and that time helps me relax. I feel refreshed, as if I were injected with energy. I pretend that therapy is my coffee, the one you drink at eight o'clock in the morning and at two o'clock in the afternoon for a jolt of energy.

I recently had a client who had many little problems with her partner; she would come and talk to me about them. She told me, "Jane, I don't know if I want to get divorced, but I think we are on that road. I feel like we're moving too fast toward a divorce." I would say, "Well, why don't you go to therapy? Look, there is individual therapy or couples' therapy. Maybe your problems are not related to your relationship; maybe they are related to work, stress, daily life... I am not a therapist, but I can suggest that you look into it. There are people specialized in this."

Time went by and she kept coming back to tell me about her problems. I asked her, "Do you remember how last month I told you to go to therapy? What happened?" She said, "Oh no, Jane, therapy is for crazy people."

But it's not like that. Therapy is very beneficial and having a person we trust to listen to us and give us advice is unmatched.

So, to my clients, I recommend seeking therapy—a psychologist, a confidant, someone you can talk to about all this and give you perspective. She asked me if I went to therapy and I told her that I did, which was one of the main reasons I recommended it to clients. I'm not going to promote something I don't believe in. She made up her mind and told me, "I'll see if I can do it then."

After a few months, she told me about more problems.

And before she continued, I asked her, "Did you go to therapy like I recommended? I remind you that this is the third time you have come to tell me about the same problem, and I have already recommended you go to therapy twice. If you think you can solve the problem by yourself, don't go, but if you insist on asking for advice, you'd better go to therapy."

The client said to me, "Oh, Jane, okay, give me the number of the therapist."

I gave her two numbers, one for a therapist and one for a psychologist. After a few months, she came to me and said, "Jane, going to therapy is the best advice you could have given me." Then, my client confessed that she had become addicted to therapy, as it gave her incredible peace and her problems had been solved in all areas.

With therapy, one can see things through a different perspective, with clarity, calmly. It is a space for relief and self-knowledge.

Therapists always inspire a lot of trust and I think that's what you need when working with people who are going through a difficult situation like a divorce.

This point of therapy goes very much hand in hand with the earlier point of getting to know yourself again. Getting back to being at peace with yourself. There are therapists of all kinds, specializing in a variety of issues. And there are a range of options, from counseling, for example, to spiritual or Christian therapy, to neurolinguistic therapy. In my case, I have taken therapy based on the identification and recognition of my past; that is, I have seen therapists who have helped me identify where and when I was hurt in the past and that has helped me a lot.

Therapists have helped me identify problems from my past. I recommend that therapy should be a tool even before divorce. For example, in the case I was telling you about, my client went to therapy, which helped her resolve the issues that had led her to think she wanted a divorce in the first place. I believe that therapy has stages, and it may be that in a given moment, you need personal therapy, and in another, marriage therapy. If you are a child, adolescent, young person, or adult, if you have children in those ages and diverse problems, therapy will be the tool that can help you through multiple situations.

So, if you ask me when you should go to therapy, I would say today, before the problems even appear. If you are already going through them, then you should go during and when you already solved them, too.

It is important to distinguish between the therapist, the psychologist, and the psychiatrist. My recommendation is that you should first seek the option of therapy. I recommend a psychologist only if in the middle of the conflict you detect thoughts of self-destruction, since this person is a little more qualified and can attend to someone who has suicidal thoughts. A psychologist can identify where these suicidal thoughts come from or where the idea of self-destruction comes from.

Therapists are there to talk to you and advise you on minor problems. You could say that a psychologist is for deeper problems, people who have hit rock bottom. And the psychiatrist, of course, would be a resource when the problem is already a mental health problem, such as schizophrenia, bipolar disorder, even insomnia or anxiety—serious problems that require medication support.

If the issue is on the depression side, it is important to see a psychiatrist, especially these days, when depression has become such a common and serious issue because recently, the diagnosis of depression has increased. The psychiatrist can contribute a great deal since depression is sometimes of a chemical nature.

In my case, I experienced depression due to hormonal issues. I started to feel very strange things in my body, and I was diagnosed with depression. In my family, there have been several cases of cancer. I have many uncles and aunts who died of cancer. My mom is a cancer survivor, and I was diagnosed with breast cancer in 2017. They removed half of my breast and gave me chemo and radiation.

I fell apart. It not only affected me emotionally, but also physically, because after all the treatments I underwent, they detected cancer in my womb, and I had to have surgery again! They discovered that the cancer had invaded the entire reproductive system; so, it was necessary to remove my womb, uterus, cervix, tubes, ovaries— everything that physically makes me a woman.

When I woke up from the anesthesia, I felt something horrible—an unsettling sensation. I did not know what was happening to me. I was trembling and crying. Then, the doctor arrived and told me, "I had to remove every-thing because everything was already invaded by cancer, and you entered what is called immediate menopause, that's why you feel this way. You are experiencing a hormonal change in your body because you no longer have ovaries that produce hormones. Your body is in shock." I had to stay in the hospital for 10 days and it was terrible.

They gave me hormone treatment to try to level off, but I couldn't stabilize myself. I would come home crying. When I finally got my hormones under control, I had to get used to the fact that my body was not going to be the same. I was on hormone treatment for four years before deciding to have breast reconstruction, but one of the two implants became encapsulated. I had to go back to the surgeon who ordered a mammogram; the result was that, again, I had tumors in the same breast.

I recently underwent surgery and those tumors have already been removed. They interrupted my hormone therapy because it was causing the cancer to come back. Today, I do not take hormones, but I still have some ailments and sweating.

Therapy continues to energize me daily and teaches me to be more attentive to my thoughts and reactions. Try to find someone who is recommended by someone you know and who is a recognized professional.

STEP 5:

START AGAIN WITHOUT FEAR

After a serious loss, such as divorce, there is always a little fear. But you should not be afraid. You have to be aware that it is possible to start again, and you have to do it without fear.

In my accounting firm, I had a couple of long-standing clients. They both came to do their taxes together, and one day, the husband died. My client and he had been married for 50 years and the case caught my attention because one day, she came to me and said, "Jane, it's just that my husband was the one who took care of everything like the cars, the bank, the house... And now, you see, it's been five years since he died, and I can't get used to doing things. I am scared of it." I looked at her and asked her sincerely, "Why are you afraid? You are still living here. What are you afraid of?" She said, "I don't know how to do it, it scares me…"

And I replied, "But what is it that you don't know how to do? Well, you are here doing the taxes, just like your husband did. You come, you sit down, and you do the taxes. Don't be afraid. You are alive."

The following year, when she came to do her taxes, she had a totally different look on her face. She was much calmer. I asked her how she had been doing and if she needed it. She said, "You know what? The last time I was here, you told me not to be afraid and I hadn't realized that even though I was afraid, I was doing things. So, I just thought to myself, *what am I afraid of?* I was doing all the things! So, I kept doing them and now, they feel very normal. I don't do them with fear, but with the conviction that I can do it! Thanks for your advice; you told me to do it without fear."

I was very pleased to have been able to help her. It was neither my job nor my intention. It wasn't planned. I didn't give her speech after speech about fear. I just told her what I saw. And it is that easy—one has to live without fear, to do things calmly, without fear that they will go wrong or that we will make a mistake. If you make a mistake, you have to be brave enough to face it and make it right.

That is living without fear. To do things with peace of mind. After this process of divorce, following all the steps above, you may still feel afraid, so I would tell you to do the following:

You're going to have breakfast alone. Have a coffee and experience that feeling of loneliness. If you don't want to be in a public place, go to a park, or go hiking. When you are alone with you, you order, your breakfast, your little egg, you'll enjoy it. You'll say to yourself, "Yes, I can. I am not afraid."

STEP 6:

LEARNING AND TRAINING

My next advice to get over a divorce is: Learn, get trained, study! After all I have experienced with my divorce and all the divorces I have seen, I know for sure that after these experiences, there is a great need to learn. It makes me hungry to learn, to study, to know how the law works. So, I give you this advice: educate yourself.

This aspect can go hand in hand with distraction because you can entertain yourself by studying or taking a course. I have another client who told me about a new partner she had. He was going through a divorce. He wanted to give her everything because he was still in that stage of falling in love. So, he said: "Hey, I would like to pay for you to take any course you want—cooking, sewing, art, whatever, because I want to give you that gift." She chose a course, finished it, and after a while, they ended their relationship.

One day, I met her, and she told me that she was no longer with that boy. I dared to ask why and she answered, "Jane, you know what? I felt that he was pushing me away, that he didn't want me to be by his side and that's why he was paying for my courses." When she told me this, I replied, "Oh wow, explain it to me. The boy was offering her the courses so that she would grow, but she took it as a punishment, as something bad, a way of pushing her away. So, I shared my perspective and told her that it was not that way.

I explained to her that, for me, if a man gave me that opportunity and gave me the chance to train and study through a course, I would have taken advantage of it because it is a way to help you grow—to make you a better person. And I will always see studying as that: a way to improve yourself.

When I gave my client this perspective, she was speechless.

She had never visualized it this way and maybe if she

had, she would still be in a relationship with that boy. I was shocked to realize how the same scenario can be so different depending on personal perspectives. What I saw as something fabulous seemed like torture to my client. You may have one perspective, but if someone opens your eyes and lets you see other possibilities, it is a way of opening your horizon, helping you focus, learn, or discover vicissitudes that change you. It is important not to lock yourself in and that is what studying is for.

The knowledge and courses that I recommend you consider are for several objectives. First, to take you away from stress during the process; they serve very well as a form of distraction. But they also help you get to know yourself.

If you take a course and learn a little more, you may discover other facets of yourself and realize how valuable you are. So, it would also be linked to the aspect of self-knowledge. With a course, you can discover that you can do more, which distracts you. It means you are no longer thinking about the divorce, the pain, or the fear. A lack of focus on the important things in life prevents you from advancing and moving to the next level. However, studying, training, and courses can be very useful in our lives.

For this reason, I congratulate you—you, who are reading these letters—because I know that you are looking for a way to get ahead. No matter what situation you are in, I know you will succeed.

Many times, I found myself in a dead-end tunnel, in situations that I thought would never end. And today, I am here, sharing all those experiences with you and giving advice to many people.

In the following points, I outline more recommendations that helped me get out of that fatal divorce. Cheer up! Keep on reading...

STEP 7:

ACCEPT
THE
ADVICE

The suggested step is this: Accept the advice and support you receive. Listen to people who have been through something similar or who have more experience than you do.

I have some experiences of people who have gone through unfortunate circumstances, precisely because they disregarded the advice of others. I had a client who was married to a policeman. He had brought her from another city.

He told her that he didn't want her children to grow up with nannies. He wanted her to dedicate herself completely to the children, which means he didn't let her work. He put her in a very nice house and told her to dedicate herself to the children, to take them to sports, to cook for them, and so on.

After 10 or 12 years, he asked her for a divorce. She didn't understand the reasons why he didn't want to be with her anymore. She said, "But why? I am the perfect wife. You told me to stay at home, you told me to take care of the children, you told me to take care of you... What happened?"

He had found someone else and that's why he wanted a divorce. Anyway, she contacted me and said, "Jane, you don't know what references I've received about you. I want you to handle my divorce." Grateful, I asked her how I could help.

She needed me to help her with the divorce, but she had some particular ideas. I said, "Well, you're my client and I'll help you through all the steps." She started telling me about it and as she was talking to me, I offered advice. Unfortunately, she threw all my advice out the window.

I told her, "Look, he has a very good lawyer. I suggest you don't make drama, don't get angry with him, and take it easy because if you cause drama, they will use it against you and instead of you getting what you want, it will hurt you in the long run."

I told her all this because I had studied at the Police Academy. There, I learned how it is possible to obtain information from people without them realizing it. There are tactics that many of us aren't even aware of. And we only realize that this has happened when we finish talking, have already said everything, and gave weapons to build the case against us.

This client listened to everything I told her and agreed that she would do it, but then she told me, "Jane, you see, he did this and that to me." I responded by telling her, "Last week, I told you not to do that and I told you to calm down. I even offered that I would answer the messages at night and tell you what you could say to use their strategies to your advantage." But she opted for a foolish attitude instead, saying: "Oh, yes, but I couldn't contain myself. I was so angry that I had to answer him at that moment." Anyway, she did not pay attention to all my indications.

This happened a few years ago. She learned the hard way

to listen to my suggestions and recommendations, as she had several consequences due to her behavior.

Currently, she has nothing to do with that man; the divorce passed, and custody remains with her. Everything is fine. Now, she tells me about her new partners and asks me, "Jane, what do you suggest? What do you advise me?"

As the saying goes, "The devil knows best for being old than for being the devil." There are many people who have been through divorces, breakups, and events of various kinds, and these people can persuade you and give you good advice. It is important that you are receptive to recognize who can give you good advice and who is giving you bad advice.

In this regard, you may also want to look for a support group for recently divorced people, so you hear other perspectives from individuals who are going through a similar situation. Unless you need other specialized help, these support groups are quite satisfying and affordable. You could also seek advice from someone impartial.

It is not as beneficial to opt for advice from family, especially if they have not lived through the divorce situation. The best thing to do is to ask an impartial and mature person, who has already had some years of experience in what it is you're going through.

I'll tell you what happened to me recently with a certain person I love very much. She has nothing to do with divorce, but I think the example I have of her explains what I mean very well about the knowledge of those who are older.

She is about 21 years old, and she recently obtained her license as a phlebotomist, a person who draws blood. With this license, she got a job at the blood bank. She has a good hand at drawing blood, which allowed her to exceed at this job. She was studying medicine and also had a very flexible schedule because she was going to university. Her job was very good because it gave her important benefits. One day, I found out that she had started seeing a boy, and therefore, she started neglecting work.

I told her, "Hey, take care of that job. Don't miss so many shifts. Pay more attention to it..." She said that she was taking care of it. After a while, she dialed me and told me very sadly, "I have been fired." When I asked her the reason, it was obvious; she had skipped too many shifts.

I felt like saying, "I told you so," but of course, I didn't. Still, she had a good job and should have taken care of it. As a result, she was crying, but that wouldn't solve her problem or remedy the situation. I suggested that she send job applications to as many positions as she could and stay in school.

I have always told that to all young people: "Stay in school. Save your money. Don't be a spender. Cover your needs first and then spend on entertainment." I asked this girl, "How is your financial situation?" and she answered, "Well, I can afford about two or three months without working." I supported her a little while she found another job, but after a few months, I had to tell her, "Although I don't want to tell you this, I have to. I warned you to take care of your previous job. I told you not to miss work and you didn't pay attention." She told me, "I know you were right."

You say what you say because you have more years and more experience. And receiving advice should not make you sad; on the contrary, it should make you feel important because it means that you are valuable and loved by someone.

If I dare to advise my clients on this or that subject, it is because I have had the experience or because I have seen similar cases. If I tell you something, it is because I have already lived it and it is a suggestion.

Before the experience, there is a long road, a journey that you have to go through and that's why people with years of experience can give you suggestions, advise you, support you.

But in the long run, you are the one who has the freedom to take the advice or not.

STEP 8:

TALK ABOUT DIVORCE WITHOUT PAIN

The penultimate step is to be able to talk about what happened without feeling pain. This means overcoming what happened to you and being able to talk about it without feeling terrible. I have seen people who, despite the years, are unable to turn the page; consequently, they cannot move forward from where they are.

If you are not able to put an end to the situation, you will remain stagnant. The situation will continue to prevent you from moving on with your life. Unfortunately, this happens to many. I have a client who has been there for I don't know how many years, with immense anger and pain for the husband she divorced.

They had five children. She was not working and while

they were still together, he met someone with whom he cheated on her. They divorced and he left her with the children. Between the pain of what happened to her and what followed, she has not been able to get over it and I find it very unfortunate because the man died, and she continues with very deep resentment.

I see her occasionally and her life is passing her by. The children are growing up and she remains absent. She has not even been able to rebuild her life. I meet her from time to time and it is always the same. She repeats her same sorrows, the same pain, and she cries about and curses her ex. That anger makes me very sad because I have advised her to get some kind of counseling and to look for help so she can get herself out of this destructive cycle.

She acted wrongly repeatedly when she separated from him; she harassed both him and the couple, even breaking into the house where they both lived. It was certainly a bad act.

I believe that the consequences of someone being stuck in pain or anger are serious, for these consequences prevent them from appreciating how beautiful life is.

Many of us are visibly aging because we give power to pain and anger to rule in us. No one comes near us because we give off a negative aura and energy. But if we allow the pain to be there, it is impossible to look forward and realize that the past is behind us and that we have overcome it. When you heal, you realize that all the painful processes are over, and it doesn't hurt anymore.

When you have gotten over the pain, then it is possible to look back and say, "Wow, it hurt me at the time, but now, I'm fine. What a wonderful lesson." When you can talk about the people who hurt you in a natural way, without crying or without feeling bad, it means that you are already healed. On the contrary, if a person has not yet healed, he or she may not be able to talk about what happened. Talking about the past without pain takes time.

It is difficult to overcome this. It's been many years since I got divorced, but I still feel some pain when I talk about him. As I was writing this, I had to remember things that were already dusty in my heart. But as I thought about them again, I realized that I still had to make an effort to contain myself. It is not as painful as it was in the beginning. Before, I definitely couldn't even talk about it because I had to take deep breaths and many times, I would cry. I had to distract myself or get a coffee because I couldn't go on.

As a friend of mine who is a psychologist says, "In order to heal a wound, you have to open it, take a small knife, and remove all the infection. Only that way will the wound heal."

I felt that when I talked about my divorce, that wound would open up, and I really didn't want that pain to come flooding in. It was only when time and the hard work of healing did its work that I was able to be at peace again, to feel my life differently. It is very important that you don't carry the pain forever.

When you give yourself that opportunity to heal, you can feel the wound and say, "This happened to me. There's the scar. I can talk about it." That scar is a reminder that you had tremendous pain and that at the time, it festered, that you had to reopen the wound and clean it out, but it's also a reminder that you are strong and capable of healing.

It is an emotional tattoo, so to speak, and then you can talk about it, look back, and know what hurt you. You can identify with others and then move on. Now, be very careful. I am not talking about the pain of loss of life, but the pain of loss of a partner because when there is a loss due to death, it is very different from the loss due to divorce. When there is a separation, it is another pain.

Being able to look back from the point of view of leaving it in the past and moving forward is essential.

STEP 9:

USE YOUR EXPERIENCE TO HELP OTHERS

In my experience, the greatest satisfaction I have obtained is being able to help people. As I have shared with you from the beginning, for me, personal peace is priceless, and today, I can feel satisfaction because the work I do also gives me the pleasure of supporting others.

Helping is about reaching into the souls of others and transforming lives. I can tell you about some stories of couples who broke up—not necessarily with formal divorces or with legal lawsuits; on the contrary, it can be that a couple is fighting or that there is someone who has a marital conflict.

And I know of cases like this that have separated after five or ten years and they never signed a paper. It is not a question of saying whether or not it is right to live that way, but legally, they are not married, period. So, there is no divorce, but they suffer the same.

The emotional consequences are identical.

The emotional process is just as hard, whether it is a legal divorce or a separation. Several people approach me who are not formally married and they seek me out because I give them confidence. I don't know if it is the tone of my voice or the way I speak, but I am fortunate that many people open up to me about their relationships.

I have clients who come for help with processes related to vehicle or tax matters and they end up telling me about their ex. It is curious that what I have lived is there, as if transmitted in my aura, and that is why they open up to me. I find that the fact that I use my personal experience is what allows people to seek me out for emotional support.

After the storm comes the calm, and after the divorce—which is a very strong experience—there remains a life experience that is powerful. People who have gone through this experience should try to use it to help others. Why? Well, because you have already gone through unimaginable pain that made you learn in the process of healing. You can support either your neighbor, your niece, your daughter, and so on, because you are able to help them with your experience. Helping one person is enough.

Your experience is yours, yes, but you should not keep it to yourself; rather, you should use it to promote fulfillment. To help others so that they can come to feel as you feel. You don't know how immensely satisfying it is to be on the other side, to feel good, and to know that you passed that storm and now you are at peace.

And it shows because on social networks, you no longer post sad or indirect things; now, you just post happy things. This is how I had that impact on that person and it feels very good. It is very satisfying and fulfilling.

If you have gone through this experience and you have followed all these steps that I share with you, surely you are already on the other side. So, I advise you not to be quiet. You don't know at what point someone can learn from your experience, and you need to use your experience to make a radical change in your life from this painful story, showing others that you were able to make a beautiful ending out of pain.

Talk about what you lived through, get it out of you—out of your mind and out of your heart. Express it. It took me four years to get started with my nine-step process because that's how long it took me to achieve zero contact. After that, it took me another few years before I was able to say without fear what happened to me.

Now, I know that if you are open to following these steps and working through the pain of the divorce process, it gets better.

Little by little, you will be able to talk about it and get it out and it will turn out to be a learning experience.

I don't believe that silence is good. To help a person, you must share your knowledge and experience. That, at the same time, helps you and heals you faster because you are building, looking forward to the future, and seeing that everything happens for a reason.

I think the fundamental thing is to share. If you followed the nine steps and they worked for you, share it with your acquaintances and friends who are going through this situation. Put it into practice and start looking at how you can bring others closer to this path of overcoming.

Talk, share, and change, only then will you be able to give back with good something of what life brought you because someone who urgently needs guidance is looking to learn from your experience.

Today, I did it, and tomorrow, it can be you. Don't give up.

Jane

CONCLUSION

Writing this book on *How to Get Over a Divorce*, took me very little time.

But to have discovered, practiced, and experienced all this information point by point and case by case has cost me many years of my life.

During this time, I came across different situations— cases that, although painful, taught me what should not happen in a divorce.

With this book, you have specific and summarized content of all those stories, situations, and years of experiences. This content can lead you to make better decisions when ending a relationship.

Now, what follows is totally up to you:

TAKE ACTION!

Maybe doubt, fear, and insecurity will start to win you over...and you turn back.

But *TODAY*, you have to take the first step.

You already know what to do.

In case you need **personalized advice** for your particular situation, you can contact me through any of the following means:

Email: velascokjane@gmail.com

WhatsApp: +1 (760) 534-0075

I would even like to bring my conference to your city.

I am only a phone call away.

JANE

ABOUT THE AUTHOR

Jane Velasco is a Divorce Counselor, Speaker, and Entrepreneur. As a bilingual counselor for many years, Jane has been helping people with their divorce processes since 2010 and has delivered talks at many conferences in several states of the United States.

She is the owner of *Xtreme Services*, a tax preparation services organization and an active participant in the AFSP (Annual Filing Season Program), a voluntary program of the IRS. She is also a Certified Immigration Consultant in the State of California, with a degree in Law Administration (Administration of Justice). Velasco is currently completing a diploma in Emotional Intelligence.

Velasco was born in Los Angeles, California, but lived

most of her childhood and adolescence in Guatemala. He currently lives in Desert Hot Springs, California, and enjoys listening to music, hiking, and traveling.

Thanks for reading!
We hope you have enjoyed
this book

The Author reads every comment posted on her Amazon page.

We would appreciate it if you shared your opinion about this work, as this will help other readers to make their own decisions to invest their own time and resources in this content.

Two things before you leave your comment:

First, we ask for only frank feedback, reflecting the true impact this book has had on you.

Second, that these comments are practical with the intention of helping others make their own decisions.

If you've enjoyed this book and want to share your thoughts with the Author as well as future readers, we'd love for you to leave a review on the Amazon page where you purchased it.

Your comments and star rating will help others discover this book and know what to expect.

Thank you for your support!

Editorial Misión

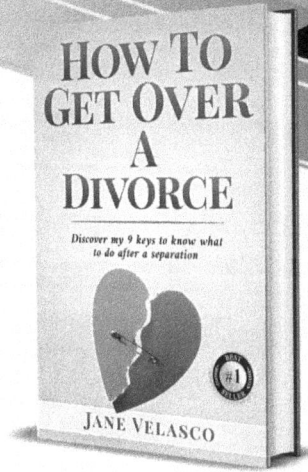

NOTAS

NOTAS

NOTAS

NOTAS

NOTAS

NOTAS

www.ingramcontent.com/pod-product-compliance
Lightning Source LLC
Chambersburg PA
CBHW071028280326
41935CB00011B/1494